Use Your

W.O.R.D.S.

Weapons Over Real-life Decisions and Situations

by

Regina Farai' Edwards

DORRANCE
PUBLISHING CO
EST. 1920
PITTSBURGH, PENNSYLVANIA 15238

Dorrance Publishing Co.
585 Alpha Drive
Suite 103
Pittsburgh, PA 15238
Visit our website at *www.dorrancebookstore.com*

ISBN: 979-8-88604-768-4
eSIBN: 978-1-6386-7677-5

Dedication

This book is dedicated to my daughter Jazzmyn Agoha. You are the reason I am still here. You are the driving force behind everything good in my life. Thank you for teaching me unconditional love, patience, resilience and true joy. I know there are a lot of things you don't understand right now, but I hope as you get older, you look back on the life we had together and you see that your mother never gave up, even in those seasons of darkness. I hope when you read this book, that if empathy develops for me, pride will quickly follow. I love you, infinity times over!

Mommy

I also dedicate this book to young Regina. You are great. I love you. There is nothing wrong with being kind and quiet, and there's nothing wrong with you. I promise to continue the journey you started.

I am not a life coach. I am someone who has gone through a variety of trials in my life, and what I've learned is life takes you through things for a reason. We must discover that reason so the journey's not in vain. I've also learned that the journey I walked was not as lonely and isolating as I thought. Someone has cried the same tears, felt the same pains and lived the same past.

This book was written with fear but also excitement. I was afraid because I had to expose areas of my life that I've intentionally hidden due to shame, regret, and fear of judgment. However, my excitement comes from knowing truth equals freedom. I'm also excited because I know sharing these experiences will let you know you're not alone and maybe something I've said can redirect your life and begin the process of healing.

In order to become the very best versions of ourselves, we must understand there's a power that already lies within. We know that when we're young. We're confident and fearless, but at some point, we lose those traits and let people and things steal our birthright.

Certain experiences can have us believing sadness, toxicity, struggle and pain are supposed to attach to our inner being. We think we're supposed to accept those feelings and become comfortable with them. That is far from the truth!

I want to shed light on issues we sometimes force ourselves to go through in darkness. If you've ever been bullied, had a secret shame you couldn't confess, a private feeling eating at you, or even moments of self-doubt and you're ready to change the trajectory of your life, I believe with all my heart this book will help you get there.

From elementary school to my thirties, I lived a quiet and introverted life that unfortunately shielded a growing depression I didn't know I had. That depression created insecurity, and insecurity birthed a personality that allowed mistreatment and abuse from others and shame and unforgiveness from myself. In self-reflection over the years, I've discovered that my words, whether in writing, spoken out loud to others or inward to myself, were the one constant thing that not only made me feel safe and secure, but also silenced the voices in my head that told me I wasn't enough.

This book unlocks the pages of my many diaries where I wrote poetry during times of pain and poured out my thoughts in trials. It shares moments where I've verbally confronted God in moment of grief, others who dishonored me and also myself for not believing and seeing the best in me.

As I share stories about my life and how I dealt with fake friends, failed relationships and wavering faith, I will expose my real thoughts and writings in those exact moments. Every word developed me and became my weapon to overcome so many hardships in my life.

My prayer is that this book really connects to you. If just one part resonates with you and encourages you to shift your mindset and use **YOUR W.O.R.D.S., Weapons Over Real-life Decisions and Situations** (and not someone else's) as tools of empowerment, then everything I went through—all the tears I cried, all the sadness I endured, and all the disappointments I experienced—would have been worth it.

Imagine this book as a conversation between friends in a safe environment. You may cry, or laugh, or high-five a friend in a moment of confirmation. Or, just maybe, this book will inspire to you write your own words and manifest the changes you want to see in your life.

Using your words as a weapon happens when you:

> 1. **Write them**, because if you keep the pain in, it will overtake you and consume you like a cancer. Sometimes you may not be ready to share with another person, but getting your feelings out of your head can make a world of difference.

> 2. **Speak them**, because life and death lie in the power of the tongue.

> 3. **Believe them**, because words, along with faith, bring about action and change.

> 4. **Share them**, because we go through things and overcome them to help the next person along the journey.

At the end of each story there's a blank page left for your words. After you read, what did you learn or feel? What goal do you need to accomplish that you've been putting off? Who do you need to verbally confront, apologize to or forgive? What doubts and insecurities about yourself need to be changed in your mind and heart? Write it down and then do it!

I have been developing a relationship with this weapon for more than twenty years. I'm still learning. Being vulnerable but also bold enough to face my fears has made such an impact in my life. My journey is not over, however. It's not neat, and it's not pretty, but it's mine. A part of my growth is to finally reveal my truths. This is my chapter four. I now pass it on to you. Do the work. Use your weapon! Use your WORDS!

God bless!

"Iron sharpeneth iron; so, a man sharpeneth the countenance of his friend."

–Proverbs 27:17

Table of Contents

Chapter One: Write your words

UGLY girl

I grew up in Green Pond, South Carolina, a small town with an average population of about 2,500 people. My grandparents' home, which was literally next door, and church were the main sources of fun for my sisters and me. Both places pretty much offered the same benefits since my grandfather was a pastor and several family members held ministerial positions.

We were always at church or my grandparents' home because:

> 1. We were a very close family who supported each other.

> 2. All of our cousins were there.

> 3. We had no choice (plus we held every position in the youth department)!

Later in life, we chose to give our lives to God and began attending church for the right reasons: gossip and drama! Just kidding... (couldn't resist) ...to serve God.

I lived a very simple and "country" life. However, the benefit of living in such a small town for a child is that you have great, long-lasting friendships because your friends were either your family or people you've lived around your whole life.

I was born in 1987. Back then, the world moved much slower. Life in the country was amazing. I couldn't imagine having any other kind of childhood. Summers playing in the neighborhood, making tree houses, riding bikes, discovering adventures in my grandfather's cow pasture, and running from the mosquito man—the man who drove a spray truck to minimize the number of mosquito's we encountered—were the best years of my life. We were so carefree, and to this day when I think back on those memories, all I can do is smile.

Although I was a quiet child, I was happy. I was confident in my life and what I would do with it. The future wasn't scary, and there was nothing I didn't believe I could accomplish.

It wasn't until I finished elementary school and had to be bussed to the next city for middle school that I was faced with…me. There, I discovered I was ugly. I was invisible. I was irrelevant. And for the first time in my life, I became aware that my family's financial status wasn't something to be proud of, and my looks didn't measure up to the world's standard of beauty.

I was a dark-skinned girl with short, brittle hair and bucked teeth developed from sucking my thumb from birth until first grade. My nail beds are hereditarily dark, and I barely have eyebrows. My knees and elbows were black from living a carefree childhood, and in addition to my physical looks, my sisters and I didn't wear the latest fashions. We were excited just to get two new outfits a piece from Walmart to wear and share for the first few days of school.

We were raised with respect and to honor the Edwards name. We weren't sassy with attitudes. We didn't disobey, and we didn't "clap back" at people. We were humble and submissive and just wanted everyone to be just as nice as we were.

The first time someone told me a person I believed to be a friend had been talking about me, it crushed me. She had talked about my clothes, my hair, the condition of the house I grew up in, and my family. I silently cried on the school bus, being sure to wipe away my tears before they fell to my cheeks so no one would notice. I could feel the wall of isolation slowly building inside of me as I looked out of the window on the way home.

But after wiping my tears, I grabbed a pencil, poured out my pain and put it into words with this poem: Me.

Me

With my short, black hair
That people call bald
My chicken pox-scarred legs
That's not very tall

I'm just living my life
Happy as can be
Doing my thang
Just being me

With my beautiful gifts
Of loving to sing
And writing of poems
To happiness it brings

It's just what I do
Anyone can see
I can be anything
Just being me

My Coca Cola shape
And nice-sized lips
My fatty fat cheeks
And wide little hips

I can fly like a butterfly
And steal honey from a bee
Just look at them haters
Eyeing me

With my so-called friends
Smiling in my face
Think I don't know they fronting
And trying to make me waste

My goodness on them
Don't need the company
'Cause I'm a magnet for friends
By just being me

It's a hard road to walk
When your name is Regina
And hear best friends say
Let her go, I don't need her

But when I look in the mirror
Do you know what I see?
A black, beautiful girl
That nobody can be but ME!

Regina (Sarai) Edwards

Me

with my short black hair
that people call bold
My chicken-pot scared legs
thats very tall.

I'm just living my life
happy as can be
doing my thang.
Just being me.

with my beautiful gifts
of loving to sing
And writing of poems
to happiness it brings

Its just what I do
anyone can see
I can be anything
Just being me.

My coca cola shape
and nice size lips.

my fatty fat checks
and wide little hip.
I can flyy like a butterfly
and steal honey from a bee
Just look at them haters
eyen me

with my so-called friends
Smilen in my face
think I don't know they fronten
and tryn to make me waste

my goodness on them
o dont need they company
cause I'm a magnetic friend
by just being me.

I hard rode to walk
when your name is Regina
and hear your best friend say
let her go I dont need her.

So when I look mirror
do you know what I see
A black beautiful girl
that nobody can be but me!

Have you ever heard the term, "fake it 'til you make it?" This poem seems like it came from a pretty confident child, doesn't it? I had to write on paper what I couldn't say to people. I had to fake confidence because now, there was a question mark where there used to be a period. "I am a pretty girl" turned into "am I a pretty girl?" This moment began an internal battle where what I was raised to believe about myself conflicted with what outsiders told me. The inner me was fighting for my self-confidence with this poem. Writing kept me sane. It became my friend, confidant and first pair of boxing gloves.

Side note: Here's something I never really paid any attention to until my adult years. It's quite funny, actually. My grandparents gave all forty-something of their grandchildren nicknames that stuck with us forever. One of my sisters was called 'Lady of the House.' One cousin was called 'Precious.' However, my nickname was '**Pretty Girl**.' I heard that every day, even from my aunts and uncles, yet I allowed other people to change the narrative. Isn't it funny how you can hear the word 'pretty' for years and experience positive treatment from family and friends, but the ONE negative thing spoken about you that grazes your ear or the ONE hurtful action is the thing that sticks, causes lasting pain, and becomes the fiber that alters your life forever? After reading my stories, I hope you can identify those moments in your own life, and choose to respond with w.o.r.d.s. that combat not only the negative actions of others but also the mental battle that awakens in your mind.

As I got older, in my teenage years, I was teased and talked about more. As the spectrum for beauty grew further from my look, and the need for friendship hierarchy grew among my peers, the more I believed I didn't fit in and the more my self-esteem dissolved. My obsession to not be seen or heard was at an all-time high. Middle school was tough, but high school was a whole new monster. At times, I closed myself off to fun, the friends I had, the family who loved me, and, worst of all, myself.

I do want to be clear; I did not go through life as a zombie. I had great friends and terrific family members. I laughed, I joked, I participated at school and I accomplished a lot as a child. I was in girl scouts, band, choir, a health occupations club and a double-dutch team. I just didn't know how to properly identify and digest hurt, and it overtook me at times, leading to depression. I guess you could say I was a functional depressed person.

5

If you asked teachers, classmates, friends and family, they'd probably say I was quiet, nice and a good friend. They'd more than likely say I was loyal, a good listener and looked out for other people. Not one person would say I was depressed, filled with hurt and completely insecure. I learned how to hide my truth in plain sight very well. I learned how to take direct insults, overhear hurtful remarks and let people walk over me all while excelling in school, still being a good friend and smiling at the same people who talked about me.

Journaling grew more important to me in those adolescent years. If I had a crush, the guy didn't know, but my journal did. If my friends made me cry at school that day, they didn't know, but the journal knew. The journal could handle my truth even if I couldn't. I could let all my frustrations and anger out on the paper and it wouldn't be disappointed in me. It wouldn't talk back. It didn't tease me. The pen became my courage. The paper was turned into whomever I needed it to be, and that's where I'd stand up for myself time after time.

Although my journal kept my emotions secret, eventually, my behavior wasn't as easily concealed. My mood at home began to change. I would come home from school, do my homework and go to bed at 5 P.M., with excuses like "I'm just tired" or "I just really like to sleep."

The more I felt like an outsider by friends, the more skilled I became at hiding my feelings, and the more my writing increased. I developed a horrible habit of protecting other people's feelings even if it meant to dishonor my own. I pretended to be okay for my friends. I pretended to just need rest at home. I even pretended when I looked in the mirror. But I couldn't pretend on the blank sheets. I had to be real.

Real

So many times, I hide the pain

On my face they see sunshine, but my soul is really rain

They're so many things inside I have bottled up

The tears in my heart is an overflowing cup

It's a heavy load to bear, and I just can't deal

So, I'm writing this to let it go; I'm telling, it's real

The things in the past are haunting me

I know I am forgiven, but I don't feel free

It hurts so bad when I know the smile is a lie

So, I go home and think about my sadness and cry

My family doesn't understand when I want to be alone

They say, "why doesn't she want to be with us?" in and awful tone

If I told them, it would be too deep to feel

I don't even bother, I just let the sadness steal

The special times with my family I'm supposed to embrace

It won't leave me alone, happiness won't show its face

My friends think they know; they nothing at all

They think I'm on top of my life

But every day I fall

Into the ocean of depression

I don't feel worthy of God's protection

It hurts when they think that I don't hear them laughing at my hair

and the things I wear

but I won't start any trouble, even though I should

Because we were always so close and lived in the same neighborhood

I know my parents don't give me everything that fancies me

But they try their best to give me what I need

The things on this paper have not even begun to open up

Regina Farai' Edwards' overflowing depression cup

The hurt eats me up like a 5-star meal

I'm just trying to be open; trying to be real

I feel

I graduated from high school in 2005 and headed to college not knowing who I was. The mental and emotional damage was done, and I didn't know how to heal or even recognize that I needed to. I was scarred deeply but thankfully, not broken. I focused on getting good grades, creating new friendships and a bright future.

I graduated from college in 2009 and by anyone's standards, Magna Cum Laude with a bachelor's in biology and a minor in chemistry would be the definition of success, but it wasn't for me. It was hard for me to see anything I did well as something to be proud of. I made myself sick trying to be perfect to prove to all those who teased and talked about me that I was worthy. I was also trying to prove it to myself. If I wasn't the first or the best or perfect, it wasn't good enough to me.

I looked up one day, and I realized I was back home in my parents' house, unable to find a medical clinic that would let me intern. I ended up working at my old high school job, Wendy's, and it was really hard to see my peers thriving and climbing the grown-up ladder of success.

To feel a bit of nostalgia, I decided to join a friend of mine at our first college homecoming event since graduating. During an event there, a guy who had expressed his interest in me throughout the years approached me and asked me to be his girlfriend. I didn't know what to say. It took me months to consider the idea but a part of me was curious. What would being someone's actual girlfriend feel like? Well, he was always respectful and thoughtful. He was cute, and we had many things in common. I couldn't see a reason not to at least see what this could be. After all, who pursues someone for four years unless they mean it?

Everything was great! We never argued. We had so much in common, and what we wanted for our lives in the future were in sync. Our families loved each other. He made me feel pretty and wanted again, and I fell in love with him fast. After a month of dating, we were engaged and five months later, June 18, 2010, I got married at the age of twenty-three. I was happy; I was in love, and I was ready to walk into this chapter of my life. Finally, it was my time for happiness, and I just knew it would last forever.

Sadly, less than five years later, January 14, 2015, I was at the courthouse, standing in front of judge, receiving my official divorce papers. What happened? What went wrong? How did we get here? Looking back now, I can honestly say we weren't ready. We weren't prepared. I thought that because I grew up in church and he believed in God, that with those foundations, nothing could go wrong.

During the early part of our marriage, I joined the military and soon after was blessed to conceive and have beautiful baby girl we named Jazzmyn Simone. From 2012 to 2014, I experienced betrayal which advanced my post-partum depression and resurfaced my feeling of loneliness. I was thirteen hours from home, no one knew what I was going through, and I had a very young daughter who needed me to be capable of providing things I did not have at the time—emotional and mental stability.

My mental health was at an all-time low. Divorce was never in the plans, but after doing all I could think of to fix things and failing, that seemed to be my only option. I felt like I waited all these years, I took my time and I was ready to be a wife. I watched several relationships from the sidelines, and I knew what to do once I was in my own—so I thought. How did I fail? Being a single mom was not what I envisioned for my life. But here I was, and I couldn't run from it.

During my divorce process, I'd be physically at work, but my mind would be a billion miles away. No one there knew what I was going through. I'd be in the parking lot sobbing uncontrollably and afterward go to the bathroom to wash my eyes until the red was gone and walk in the office as if nothing was wrong. I'd be in briefings pretending to take notes, but really writing my thoughts. I had to get it out.

My support system, my family, was in South Carolina, and I wasn't ready to tell them I had failed at marriage. I was embarrassed, ashamed and confused. One minute I could see the marriage surviving all the trauma, the next, I was sure it was over. I didn't talk to anyone about what was going on in my home or in my head. I'm sure I would have gone crazy if I didn't get it out my head. So, here is what I wrote:

> Im Sad
> Im Confused
> Im angry
> Im dissappointed
> Im tired
> Im worried
> Im lonely
> Im different
> Im dissappearing
> Im prayful
> Im hopeful
> Im desperate
> Im sorry
> Im sad

Honesty is really the best policy. If you can't admit (at least to yourself) the raw, uncut truth of how you feel and really get in touch with your emotions—even if it is anger, regret or sadness—then the cancer of depression will continue to grow. Those fourteen lines helped me to not internalize my pain. Marriage had magically caused me to forget all the past hurt I buried, but divorce brought it back to the surface. By releasing my pain on paper, I was not only able to refocus at work, but also redesign what the new normal of my and my daughter's life was going to be. Turn your words into your weapons over your pain. It will be the beginning of your healing process.

Nighttime thoughts

Because my marriage was my only real experience in a relationship, I thought four months would be enough time to grieve my four-*ish*-year marriage and move on. I thought I had been mentally and physically preparing myself during the last two years of marriage for the potential and inevitable end. *Silly* me.

I began dating again. With one relationship which led to a marriage under my belt of experience, I thought I was more than equipped to identify any red flags and choose wisely. *Oy vey!*

As time passed, I began entertaining and dating a few men, but had no successful relationships. For six months, I dated a guy who was four years younger than I was. He took me to meet his family, but broke up with me the next month. He never intended to be serious. He wasn't looking to jump into a serious role with a single mom. I was just fun in the meantime.

I also met a guy who played it cool as if I meant nothing to him. He only pretended to value my time when I no longer made it available to him. When I decided to move on, all of a sudden, his supposed hidden feelings came to the surface. (Play JoJo's "Too Little Too Late".)

I later met a soldier boy (he was literally a soldier in the Army) who said all the right things, did all the right things, and expressed his desire for us to be in a commitment relationship, but for some reason, he never took that step. And ironically, he ignored me and disappeared when I took the initiative to pursue him.

Lastly, I met a man who lied for a year and a half about his name, age, marital status, his children, and his occupation. And oh, by the way, he stole my identity (emotionally and financially). More to come on this guy.

I know you must be thinking, "Whew girl! You need to choose better men." And you might be right, but when your self-esteem is that low, even when you want to and your friends tell you what they see, it's just really hard to move past your desire to be loved.

When I look back, however, all those experiences lead me here—to wisdom, freedom, peace and healthy relationships with first myself and then others. And I must also state, in the midst of these men, there were sprinkles of refreshing experiences that just didn't work out for amicable reasons. But with the more consistent pattern of disingenuous men, I started believing I wasn't good enough or worthy to be treated the way I saw other women treated. I started believing not only was my face not attractive but neither was my personality. People seemed to benefit from my existence because they got exactly what they needed from me—my time, energy, resources, kindness and my body—but offered nothing in return and didn't stick around long enough to get to know Regina.

This was confusing for me. Why was I attracting these types of people in my life? Why did I accept unhealthy relationships? Why couldn't I stand for my standards? What are my standards? These questions lived in my thoughts. In one of my sleepless nights, I meditated on these questions for hours and put my thoughts on paper:

Loyalty. Complete, unflawed loyalty.

A virus that infected me since birth

But its worth, seems to be more of a blessing and a curse.

A blessing for my counterparts,

because their hearts

were always protected, never neglected.

I'm always rejecting advances

and 2nd chances

to rekindle old flames, but am I the blame?

For the curse of this loyalty

Is that I get the reverse of his loyalty.

It seems nice because twice he posted us on the book of many faces,

and praises of family and friends come our way.

They smile as they say… don't they look happy!

And sadly, I am happy.

But is that an oxymoron?

Or am I just a moron who obviously doesn't know a good thing when she's got it?

I mean, it's good… I can't deny it.

But my sadness comes from his nighttime thoughts.

The things that haunt

my longing wants.

The things that go click in the night.

That's right!

Click, not bump.

Because a bump is loud and sudden. But a click is slick and hidden.

It waits for loyalty to get tired,

then it rewires

and resets.

The mind forgets he's happy.

And now weak with loyalty asleep,

he awakens his dear friend, past.

History that wasn't supposed to repeat itself

begins to go down memory lane,

and unashamed,

he flirts

with the possibilities…

Far enough not to cause visible pain,

but close enough to enjoy all he has to gain

from the exes, and nextes

and the ones-who-got away,

and the ones who wished he stayed.

Never thinking, "I went too far".

Because it's not a kiss, it's just a wish.

Not penetration

Just the sensation

of knowing

he could have it if he wanted.

But all the while, loyalty sleeps in a fairytale that never existed

where she gets what she wish,

and someone can be

just as loyal to she.

WAKE UP GIRL,

because boys will be boys,

and play with their toys.

But I wasn't aware that I had plastic hair,

and my heart could be Doc McStuffined back to pieces

after he was done Dragon Ball Z'ing my emotions!

But if the tables were turned, would it hurt?

Would it provoke you to know that loyalty got a coat

to cover up that medicated heart she wears on her sleeve?

Because believe it or not,

two can play this game and loyalty is smart.

Don't get it twisted, she's not as soft as you think.

But then again, she is loyal.

So instead of reviving relationships already sealed with goodbyes to good guys

who couldn't choose one, who couldn't be done with the single life,

Compromise wasn't an option because the clubs were always poppin',

And he had to be there…

And sweared

it was guy's night

but the highlight was Vanessa and Nicole.

The goal was never a relationship

and the realization of it hurts.

So instead of doing all that again,

while knowing the end

before it begins,

she'll just curl up on her couch, pour her thoughts out

and write a poem about a fairytale relationship

that will never be birthed in her reality.

Night Time Thoughts   10-18-15

Loyalty - Complete unflawed loyalty.
A vine ~~bad been~~ infected ~~with~~ since birth, but
it's worth seems to be a blessing + a curse.

blessing for my counter parts b/c there hearts
are always protected, never neleceted.

Im always rejecting advances + 2nd chances
to rekindle an old flame, but am I the blame
for the curse of this loyalty ~~this~~ which is that I get always
the reverse of this loyalty.

It seems nice b/c twice he posted a picture of us
on the book of many faces and praises of family
and friends come our way... they smile as
they say, don't they look happy.

~~And~~ And sadly I am - happy.
                    how can I be
But ~~why~~ Sadly happy? is that an oximoron?
Or ~~a~~ Just a moron who obviously doesn't know
~~of~~ mine when she's got it?..
~~to mean~~ means, it is good, I can deny it.

~~But~~
My sadness comes ~~to~~ from his night thoughts time
the things that haunt ~~my dreams~~ ~~my dreams are~~
~~schemes that~~ I can ~~see~~ go click in the the thing that
night ... that right click not bump ~~keeps~~
~~I know that~~ ~~deep thoughts~~ ~~slither down~~
b/c a bump is loud + sudden. But a click
slick and hidden. It waits for loyalty to get
tired and the rewires and ~~resets~~ ~~made~~
~~delete close to the key~~. Then the mind forgets
he's happy and now weak w/ loyalty asleep
It awakens it's dear friend past. History
that wasn't suppose to repeat itself, begins to
go down memory lane and ~~again~~ unashame he flirts
with the possibilities, ~~try because~~ not to cause
visible pain but close enough ~~to enjoy~~ all he has to
gain from the ex's and the next's and the
one's who got away and the ones he wished
had stayed.. Never thinking I went to far, b/c
it's not a kiss Just a wish, not penetration
Just the sensation of knowing he could have it
if he wanted.
But all the while loyalty sleeps in fairy tale
that never exist, where she gets what she wish +
someone can be Just as loyalty to she. Wake up
~~you didn't know what this person started~~
~~girls~~ love boys will be toys and play

~~trip~~ I wasn't aware that I had
plastic hair and my heart could be
doc mc stuffined back to pieces after
he was done dragon ball zing my emotions.
But if the table were turned, would it hurt,
would it ~~because you~~ provoke you to know that loyalty ~~had~~
~~rekindle~~ ~~chances + exceptions~~ ~~the one you~~
~~~~ ~~thought she was~~ ~~a heart breaker~~
got a coat to cover up that ~~heart she~~
medicated heart she was wearing on her sleeve
b/c believe it or not two can play this game
and loyalty is smart. don't get it twisted,
she's not as soft as you think.

But then again, she is loyal, so instead
~~of~~ ~~~~ ~~replaying arm of her past~~
~~~~ ~~~~
~~~~ ~~~~ ~~have~~
~~opening~~ tired on the recycling bin of
reviving relationships already ~~ended~~ w/ goodbyes to goodbyes
who couldn't choose one ... who couldn't be done by simple lies
compromise misery an option b/c the steps was struck power
and he took to be there, and swooned it was guy night but
the highlight ~~~~ ~~~~ was kareoke, and alcohol...
~~the goal was never a~~ ~~marriage~~
~~relationship and the realization of it hurts.~~
so Instead of doing all that again and knowing the end
before it begins, she'll Just curls up on her couch and
write a poem about the fairytale relationship
that will never be born in her reality.

As you look back throughout this chapter, what is your heart telling you? What do you need to get out of your head onto paper? What do you need to say to someone but can't form the words or develop the courage to do it in person? Begin by being honest with yourself first! Truth is freeing. Release is healing. Courage is empowering. Use this time to write down what your heart is feeling right now. This is the beginning of you creating your weapon!

What will you write?

_____

_____

_____

_____

_____

_____

_____

_____

_____

_____

_____

_____

_____

_____

_____

_____

_____

_____

_____

_____

_____

_____

_____

_____

_____

_____

_____

_____

Chapter Two: Speak your words
Yes, you hurt me
"Your family reminds me of the *Cosby Show*."

My childhood friends always marveled at the impenetrable bond my family seemed to have. I was also sold on the concept. My parents and their siblings raised their children with strong family values. We were cousins, but we were also brothers and sisters. I can't tell you how many times I was told my family reminded someone of the *Cosby **Show*** (not the person).

Just like most African-American families, our grandmother was the thread that held everything together. Her health slowly declined after my grandfather passed in 1999, so my family moved in with her, and we, along with a family friend, became her primary caretakers. In time, Grandma went from having a stroke and not being able to walk, talk, or feed herself, to a full recovery in a year's time. We were so proud of her and cherished our time with her until she left us in August 2001.

Our entire family grieved for a long time. We would try to come together and replicate the atmosphere Grandma created, but it wasn't the same. Holidays weren't as happy. House visits weren't as fun. It was never the same, but the love and unity we grew up having was still there and to my knowledge, would always be.

The next few years, however, taught me that people do change, blood is not always thicker than water, and families can fight and fall apart. The Cosby experience was over.

That saying "hurt people, hurt people" is very true. There wasn't one particular event or person that was the sole catalyst of the deterioration of our strong family unit, but anger, misinformation and the lack of communication caused a lot of unnecessary discord.

My sisters and I were in high school and college during this time. Being that we had not committed any misdeeds against the family, it was very confusing as to why we were being talked about, shunned, and lied on. It was a heart-breaking and very numbing experience.

Throughout those years, I tried to ignore hurtful actions. I still tried to show up, support family events and pretend I wasn't in pain when no one seemed to care. However, I was getting to the point where I no longer cared. "It is what it is," became the theme for me and my sisters.

One day in 2011, however, an opportunity was presented by an aunt to let go of all the pain from this drama, and I took it. It had been ten years since my grandmother died and about five years since our *Cosby Show* was canceled. I had graduated from college and was newly married. I was moving to Arkansas on military orders, and that day was actually one of my last days in South Carolina.

My aunt I.V. approached me, my sisters and another cousin at our grandparents' home where we were still living. She wanted to know why we act the way we did toward our family and why we distanced ourselves. She went to each person individually, asking if she had personally done something to hurt us. Everyone who was asked said no—except me.

I replied, "Yes, you and others have hurt me. Getting calls while I'm in college and saying hurtful things wasn't right! Being exiled isn't right. Spreading lies wasn't right, and it hurt. What did we do so bad that caused this?"

She let me get it all out. I was angry and it showed. More than five years of pain was finally released! I was finding my voice, and it felt good. As I spoke, my sisters and cousin nodded in agreement. Eventually, they began speaking their own truths about the hurts they felt over the years.

Once we were done, my aunt apologized. Aunt I.V. explained that she was hurt as well because of a decision my father, her brother, decided to and had the right to make. And although it was his choice, it still created pain and offense. She said we all needed to get things off our chests and talk about it so we could move on, and that day, that's exactly what we did.

I can't speak for anyone else who was there, but I felt that we had a better relationship moving forward. I let it all go, and so did she. The forgiveness was completely given and received on both sides. It felt real again. I had a piece of my family back. I had a lot of my peace back. She said she would keep in touch and she honored that.

When I became pregnant later that same year in 2011, she was actually the first person to know. She called me on a day I wasn't feeling well, and she immediately asked if I was pregnant. At the time, I didn't think I was, but she urged me to take a test and she would call back to find out the results. She actually called back, and I was pregnant! It was a very touching experience. It made me feel so good to know she cared enough to follow up and follow through!

The following summer of 2012 taught me that life is short, and it is vital that you speak what's really on your heart. I was driving with my eight-month-old daughter in the car, and John Mayer's "Say What You Need to Say" began to play on the radio. I broke down in tears. It was tears of deep sadness but also great joy because, had I not said what I needed to, I would have never gotten another opportunity to do so. My Aunt I.V. suddenly passed away from cancer in her forties, and it was very unexpected. Once again, our family was faced with grief, but one thing that gave me peace was knowing that I didn't leave things unresolved.

If there is anything weighing on your heart, big or small, don't hesitate to get it right. Life is precious. If it matters to you, say it.

Here are some of the lyrics from that song:

'Have no fear for giving in
Have no fear for giving over
You'd better know that in the end
It's better to say too much
Then never say what you need to say again

Even if your hands are shaking
And your faith is broken
Even as the eyes are closing
Do it with a heart wide open'

Say what you need to say, say what you need to say
Say what you need to say, say what you need to say'

That experience changed me in every way imaginable. Losing a family member put it all in perspective for me. Writing my feelings on paper *only*, although a good start, was no longer good enough. I owed it to myself to tell people my truth. I owed myself the opportunity to fully release. It doesn't matter if you're telling someone they hurt you or they helped you, you love them or you forgive them. Give people your truth, but what's most important is remember to speak the truth to yourself first!

Identity Theft/Time to TELL (silence kills)

In 2016, I met a man, a charming man. We'll call him Hollow. He was literally tall, dark and handsome. Something about him made me feel safe. He looked the part and played the part even better. He had everything on my checklist and more. He portrayed himself to be a caring, Godly father of *one* child who was financially stable. Hollow had his own business, a seven-bedroom home, and three brand new cars.

We got to know each other for a few months. He wined me. He dined me. He was persistent in having me. Because there was nothing materialistic I could give him that he couldn't achieve on his own, I felt that he wanted me for me.

Looking back, there were early warning signs, but I ignored them. I ignored them long enough for my feelings to justify his behavior. Months in our relationship, the verbal abuse began. He would make me feel stupid, yelling and cursing at me like I was one of his employees or subordinates. He tried to educate me on "street smarts," but when I questioned his methods or disagreed with anything, he blew up and talked down to me.

I ended things, but shortly gave in to him by talking myself into believing the disrespect wasn't that bad.

One night, he took me out to dinner and later to a hotel because his home was "under construction" and there was no electricity. We began making out and he got on top of me. He told me he loved me and proceeded to be intimate with me.

He began saying things like, "I want you to have my baby."

I began saying *stop*. I told him to get off of me. I repeated that I wasn't on birth control, and begged him not to do this.

"Stop! Get off me!"

Hollow did exactly what he said he would do and I was physically powerless to stop him. I immediately got emotional and asked him why. He said he loved me and to chill out and then he went to sleep. Not once did I identify that moment as rape, as a stolen choice or a disrespectful disregard to my request. I immediately blamed myself, let him off the hook, cried internally and prayed to God I wasn't pregnant.

After the longest two weeks of my life, waiting for my cycle to come and being disappointed, I took a test, and found out I was pregnant. I was devastated. I was scared. I was embarrassed. I was angry. I didn't know what to do. So, I made the hardest decision in my life, and at four and a half weeks, I terminated the pregnancy.

Right then I lost another part of my identity—moral integrity.

I dealt with it without Hollow. I never wanted to see or hear from him again. I blocked him, blocked out the devastation and deployed to Afghanistan shortly after.

While in Afghanistan, I tried to do some self-love work. I meditated on scriptures and practiced virtues, but there was one I couldn't master—forgiveness. I couldn't forgive myself. Why didn't I get up? Why didn't I leave? Why did I take him back in the first place? Why didn't I think of the Plan B?

The guilt from my secret termination weighed me down. I felt like the worst person in the world. Dirty. Unworthy. This was an act that could not be undone. I wasn't a good person anymore. Never in a billion lifetimes would I imagine me living this life. I didn't know how to move on. I couldn't move on.

Everything about my deployment taught me lessons about life and started to show me who I was. Yes, after all these years, I still didn't know.

I arrived in Afghanistan very burdened with guilt, but God placed amazing people in my life there to help me start a journey I am still on today. They didn't know that just by being real and speaking life into me that it was shifting the course of where my life would go after I left. I was finally taking steps to healing.

As the time drew closer for me to return home, I reflected on both the hard and wonderful moments in Afghanistan. They gave me an appreciation of life—my life, the lives of service members that were taken, the lives of those still here, and the lives of those I cared about at home.

The closer I got to arriving home, the more I began thinking about my past and the man who changed my life forever. I never told him I went through with the procedure and my guilt had me feeling like I owed him that information.

I sent him a text, told him I was back, and stated that the procedure was done. He immediately called me, apologized, and asked if we could start over. I successfully brushed him off for weeks, but again, Hollow was charming and persistent. Trauma can sometimes bring you closer to a person and make you feel like because you've been through something difficult together, you have a special bond. Plus, "he loved me" and unfortunately, I loved him too.

We began dating again, and for a whole year he spun me in a web of lies, deception and manipulation. I was completely under his control. My esteem was fragile. I was more insecure now than I was as a child. I couldn't see the truth because my spiritual vision was so fogged with hurt.

He conned me into using money I saved from my deployment and purchasing a $30,000 RV. Then he stole it. He manipulated me into giving him half of my overseas earnings for other reasons. And while I was falling in love, he was collecting my information to later steal my identity.

I cried just about every night for three months straight. Once again, I couldn't believe this was my life. The quiet girl who never bothered anyone, who didn't have a boyfriend until her early twenties, who tried to live right and follow rules…this was me? I didn't want to live. I wanted to erase the story of my life because it wasn't what I thought it would be. It wasn't who I worked so hard to become. Once again, I went to work every day, and no one knew. I tried to be brave for my daughter who was five-years-old at this time, but it was really hard.

The greatest thing in the world happened to me, however. I received orders to leave Arkansas and move to Maryland. It couldn't have come at a greater time. With God's help, I would now be able to physically and emotionally separate from this man. This move gave me the courage to disconnect at least physically (cutting the spiritual ties was a whole other story). I ended things for good as I prepared to start a new chapter for my life and new path of healing for my heart. Although I felt free from him, I still wasn't brave enough to confront him about the financial, emotional and spiritual things he had stolen from me. I figured, in time I could face him, but for now at least I was gone and could pick up the broken pieces and "*peaces*" of me.

My new life was great. I was healing. I was doing more inner work. I dated myself. I loved on myself and my daughter. I laughed. I was enjoying life. I was enjoying peace. It was beautiful.

However, five months into my new job, I received a notification from the credit bureau saying that I had a $60,000 loan added to my reports. He had used my information and purchased a truck!

My anxiety skyrocketed. This nightmare just wouldn't end. Why wouldn't he leave me alone? Why was this happening to me? I immediately called to confront him. Of course, he lied and began to threaten and verbally abuse me. He said it was my fault. He said if I went against him, I would fail. He told me to remember that my life was not the only life I needed to worry about. He also told me he was connected to people who could break into my car and place drugs or worse, a bomb inside.

I didn't realize then what I know now. It was all a scare tactic. Hollow knew something I didn't. My words had power. I didn't even think about reporting him. I had forgotten who I was so bad that defending myself against harm was not an option that naturally came to mind.

He knew as long as I believed his threats, he had my power, but if I combated him, his world would come tumbling down. For months, he won. I kept my mouth shut and tried to plead with him to remove my information, but he continued to refuse and threaten me. I prayed for this to end, hoping God would perform a miracle for me, and I'd wake up from this terror.

I contemplated settling on not doing anything because, at the moment, he was actually paying the $1,000 bill for the truck he purchased. I didn't want to piss him off because if I did, he could stop paying and there would be no way I could afford that bill with my other responsibilities.

My abnormal levels of anxiety, stress and now increasing number of reoccurring dreams about death scared me enough to FINALLY seek a counselor and confide in my sisters, Catana, Ebone' and Barbara, and best friend, Mimi. This was the first time anyone knew about what I was suffering through. I finally began speaking my truth. I told them everything. They loved on me and gave me the support I was missing out on by holding all my burdens hostage. They encouraged me to fight, but I still wasn't sure if I could.

I completed an identity theft package, but was terrified to mail it off, so I didn't. The reasonable doubt came again. "What if he *is* capable of harming me? What if he lies and makes it look like I had something to do with it? I'm not strong enough to fight him."

Yet again, God, in all his infinite glory, came in to help me be brave. He led me to a message on YouTube. I scrolled through the home page and saw the title, '*Silent Killers.*' I immediately clicked on it, and Pastor Dr. Dharius Daniels from Change Church in Ewing, New Jersey preached directly to my soul. He talked about how sometimes people steal your voice, and through fear or shame, we allow them to keep it. He said,

> *"We don't get what we deserve; we get what we tolerate. People will go as far as you let them. At some point you have to believe in your future and your destiny enough to fight for it. You have to fight not only for yourself, but for your children and the people whom you have no idea will be impacted by your journey."*

At 9:46 P.M. that night, I realized that I had a doormat personality, and the reason why this man did what he did and why other people in my life mistreat me is because I had given them permission to do so. It was easy. I never even put up a fight. But hearing those words, along with being so tired of letting those people win, I decided to never be a doormat again. Too much rode on my journey for me to just sit back and let other people create my story. I now hold the pen, and *I'm* writing the chapters!

The next day, I was focused and I knew what I had to do. I gathered my paperwork and made plans to go to the legal office and police station. However, my heart didn't match my mind, and I was still afraid. His threats played in my head over and over. I contemplated my options once more. What would happen if I lose? How can I afford another bill? I went back home with the report in my hand.

In my sadness, I went back to YouTube hoping God would speak to me again and I was directed to yet another sermon from Dr. Daniels, titled, *'Go Back and Get It.'*

The message was sterner that night, as if God Himself was telling me to GET IT TOGETHER. YOU KNOW WHAT NEEDS TO BE DONE!

Pastor Daniels said:

> *"I've got news for you: you've been robbed. Good thieves can pick your pocket, and you won't even know it until you're looking for it. Some of you didn't even realize your strength was gone until you got into a season where you needed it, and it wasn't there. [Satan] is a thief without conscience. Whatever he stole will not be returned; it must be reclaimed! You'd better go back and get it. Stop waiting for stuff to magically reappear. Here are your marching orders: stop having a pity party, waiting on a thief to gain a conscience. Take your rightful place and go back and get it. It's not coming back. It will only come back once you make a decision that you are tired of living without it."*

I felt every word. It angered me. It woke me. It changed me. And I was ready. I reviewed my complaint and mailed the package off to begin the investigation the next day. The moment the package left my hand and went into the mailbox, a freedom and feeling of peace consumed my body. He no longer had my mind. He no longer had the power. I took it back!

I knew that moment would change everything. Taking action gave me the strength to regain control of every aspect of my life. It gave me the confidence to know that I could do it. I had 100 percent of my faith toward a victory, and every day as I waited for results, I carried myself as if it was already done.

A month later, while reviewing my finances, I noticed my debt had gotten significantly lower. I thought, "this couldn't be what I thought it was." I went to my credit report and the $60,000 loan was removed! I was crying and shaking because I felt like my life had been given back to me.

I filed three police reports on Hollow. He is currently running and hiding from law enforcement. Who knows if he'll ever be arrested and held accountable for not only what he's done to me, but to all the innocent victims he affected. But what I do know is, *I* am free of him. I took my life back, and every lesson I was able to learn from the very hard times with this man will not go in vain. It has made me a better person, mother, girlfriend, businesswoman, and, most importantly, judge of character.

Don't remain silent! Silence kills. It kills your spirit. It kills your voice. It takes away the opportunity for you to free yourself of guilt and shame. Join me in breaking free today!

After reading the stories in this chapter, what is your heart telling you to say out loud? What's the thing you haven't spoken out of fear? What's the secret you don't want to reveal? Who's the person who need to say "I love you" or "I forgive you" to? Don't let another day go by without saying it. Take a few moments, gather your thoughts and reveal to yourself first the things you need to say out loud. Trust me, it is scary because you can't guarantee how it turns out, but what is guaranteed is that you are no longer held hostage by it.

What will you speak?

_____

_____

_____

_____

_____

_____

_____

_____

_____

_____

_____

_____

_____

_____

_____

Chapter Three: Believe your words

What's in a name?

It is quite interesting how the names I was given at birth were completely contradicted by everything I use to believe about myself. Remember, in the first chapter I mentioned my family called me Pretty Girl, but my whole life I believed I was ugly. I contradicted what was literally and spiritually being spoken to me.

But once my mind was clear from toxic relationships, I was able to remember who I was, who created me and what that meant. This is my name:

Regina is a Latin feminine name meaning **Queen.**   (Look it up. It really does ☺)

Why did I ever walk with my head hanging low? I was convinced my worth was way below its actual value. I was drained of my confidence, and pride was never instilled properly.

Farai' is an African name meaning ***Don't Worry, Be Happy or Rejoice***! All I have done throughout my life is worry based on other people's actions or opinions, which developed a life of anxiety.

Edwards is a surname, meaning, **son/daughter of** Edward. Edward means **prosperous guardian.**

Allow me to reintroduce myself to you. I am a queen who will not worry but rejoice because my father is a prosperous guardian!

This is how I will live from now on. This is the energy I want to radiate. I will only answer to the name of power, positivity and purpose. If someone who desires to be in my life does not add to that energy, I no longer have anything for them. I have no space, time or resources to share, and neither do you! What's your name? What will you answer to?

Affirmations (10 Things I love about me)

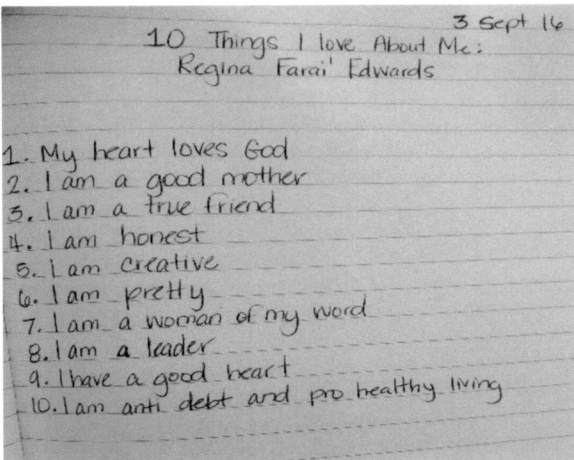

The *Merriam-Webster Dictionary* says to affirm is to state positively, to show or express a strong belief in or dedication to and to testify or declare. Affirm is a verb, which means it requires action.

As the introverted and insecure girl that I grew up to be, I never practiced this verb on myself, but I was everyone else's biggest cheerleader. I always doubted myself due to years of buying into the negativity that surrounded me and told me I wasn't enough.

I was a good writer and singer, graduated within the top 10 percent of my high school class, graduated magna cum laude from college, served my country, and was successfully co-parenting an amazing little girl, but none of that made me feel like I had anything to be proud of.

I had become so used to deflecting positivity that I couldn't recognize when someone gave me a compliment. Once, in 2016, a friend, Monisha, complimented me, and because I was so used to seeing good things for others but not me, I thought she was speaking of someone else. Noticing that, she told me to write down ten things I loved about myself and to text her a picture of what I had written when I finished. It took me an hour to put one thought on the paper. Every time I came up with something, I found a reason why I shouldn't write it. Although I had progressed and became confident enough to speak up *for* myself, a part of that speaking I developed, was negativity *against* myself. I no longer needed fake friends to tease me because I was beating them to it in my head. I no longer required men to treat me the way I deserved because I didn't feel worthy of that treatment.

After I mustered up ten things, I read them to myself and then sent them to my friend. She cheered me on and reaffirmed what I had sent. The problem was, I never affirmed it myself because I didn't believe it at all.

I stared at that sheet, trying to force myself to believe the words, but my head was too muddy. There was too much pain, insecurity and guilt in me to ever believe I possessed something worth truly loving, even though I had several family members and friends who loved me dearly.

The mind can be your master if you let it. It can train you to forget all the good in life and focus on the little that goes wrong.

While I was in Afghanistan on my deployment in 2017, I began talking baby steps trying to learn how to love. I started this lesson with reading the Bible more. Although my faith in God was always there, it wasn't as solid as it needed to be. So, when I wasn't in helicopters, documenting meetings with government and military leaders, or donning protective gear, I was reading, meditating, studying and practicing to be a better me.

Forgiving myself was the first task. I practiced 1st Corinthians 13:4-8. "Love is patient, kind, it does not envy, it does not boast, it is not proud. It does not dishonor others, it is not self-seeking, it is not easily angered, it keeps no record of wrongs. Love does not delight in evil but rejoices with the truth. It always protects, always trusts, always hopes, always perseveres. Love never fails."

The person who needed to benefit from this growth and receive this grace and love first was me. I gave myself permission to feel sad about the things that happened to me and the actions I was guilty of, but I also allowed myself adequate time to let it go and move on.

In doing these things, for the first time since I was a playful, little church girl from Green Pond, South Carolina, I began to slowly fall in love with myself just the way I was.

Because I still didn't have all the tools and the discipline to continue to reinforce the self-love, I would look up YouTube affirmations and listen to them in the morning and before bed to build up my mental strength. I would repeat them until I was able to recite them on my own. But now, I have enough in me to affirm myself!

I look back at how empty I was spiritually, emotionally and mentally, but seeing where I am today, I've made a vow to never go back, and I won't!

Affirmations (Fortune cookie)

Self-doubt and insecurity were two of the biggest mountains I've had to climb in my life. Even now. It doesn't matter how hard I prepare for something, the voice in my head telling me," I can't," or "what if," always tried to drown out my spirit telling me "you will" and "why not." That voice has stolen many opportunities from me because I believed the fear instead of my faith.

In the military we must earn our promotions through displaying a high level of knowledge in your position, as well as overall organizational knowledge. Basically, we're tested. Additionally, everything we do within a year is noted on a performance report. That report is included in the decision. Staying stagnant is not an option for my career. Elevation and steady progression are expected and enforced.

Having high anxiety and extreme insecurities but also always wanting to do my best made me a wreck during evaluations. Not only would I overstress, but I would also make it worse by putting the highest expectations on myself. I made an inner expectation to always be promoted at the first available opportunity every time. Why do we do things like that to ourselves?

I studied for months. I didn't hang out with anyone. I even explained to my daughter that playtime would have to be sacrificed most days and weekends, because Mommy had an important test to study for that would eventually make our lives just a little bit easier.

Well, that day came. I was nervous, but I felt good because I knew I studied sufficiently. However, during the test, I second guessed myself. I erased answers and questioned everything I studied. I left that exam room with mixed feelings. I began telling myself, "If I don't make it this time, it's okay. This is my first time after all."

I lost confidence, and I needed to psyche myself out of feeling disappointed if I didn't make it.

The results would be posted four months after I tested. As the release date drew near, the nerves kicked into a higher level of anxiety.

Unfortunately, my name was not on the list for promotion. I missed it by twelve points, which is a lot.

I was sad, embarrassed and felt below average. The reverse psychology I attempted did not work at all. I was hurt. I was supposed to make it. What did I do wrong?

In an attempt to make sense of this disappointing day, I went home, sat in silence and ordered myself and my daughter some takeout. Little did I know, that meal would have a small item that would make one of the biggest impacts on my resilience.

I opened the first fortune cookie I touched, just as my sisters and I used to do when we were kids. Once you have one, you can't trade it because that fortune is for you. I now continue that tradition with my daughter.

In the midst of my sadness, I opened the cookie and it said: "You will pass a test that will make you happy and more financially stable."

I thought to myself, "Hmm. Interesting. I think I'll hold onto this one."

I kept it at home for a while, but I thought I might lose it, so I took it to work and taped it to a coffee mug that held all my pens.

Every day, for the next year leading up to the next opportunity to promote, that statement was present and stayed in my subconscious thoughts.

I started studying affirmations and how powerful the mind is when it comes to not only what you believe, but what you do.

For example, when it was placed on my heart to write this book, my mind kept asking, "Who am I to write a book? It won't go anywhere. This is just another time-wasting hobby that I'm going to start, but never complete." If I would have entertained those negative thoughts like I did in my youth, you would not be reading this and hopefully receiving the help I was meant to provide you.

There are times when you have to fight and train yourself to unthink the way you've been thinking for years. Now I know that sounds crazy, like your mind is a tiny person in your head you have to battle, but it's true. There would be times where I would have to say out loud to myself, "Stop thinking that, Regina! Just stop!"

To get ahead of my own mind, I started affirming greatness to myself. I would put little subtle words and phrases on sticky notes and place them on my headboard, bathroom mirror, my daughter's room, my work notebook and the lock screen of my phone to encourage me throughout the day. I also changed my name in my phone to Tech Sgt. Edwards, which was the rank I was striving to achieve. I wrote a personal affirmation that I read every day before I studied, and placed the promotion rank on my desk so I could see it.

A year later, walking out of that same exam room, I smiled. To be honest, I felt like I knew more the previous year, but my attitude was different. I didn't doubt myself. Whichever answer came to mind first, I stuck with it. When I got to my car, I grabbed my phone and made a video that said:

"Today, I took my test. I feel great! I did great. Mark my words, my name will be on the promotion list this time."

And it was!

I was so thrilled! This practice of affirming became a part of my daily life. My best friend, Mimi, and I practice affirming each other, and if we notice anyone of us speaking negativity, we call it out and reverse the energy. I've also begun affirming with my daughter.

I affirm that my finances are above and beyond what I need. I affirm that I am healthy in spirit, body, mind and soul. And I affirm that everyone reading this will begin to affirm what they need in life.

If you have to get in the ring and fight for the freedom against negative thoughts, then do it. Please do it. You will not be disappointed. I affirm that!

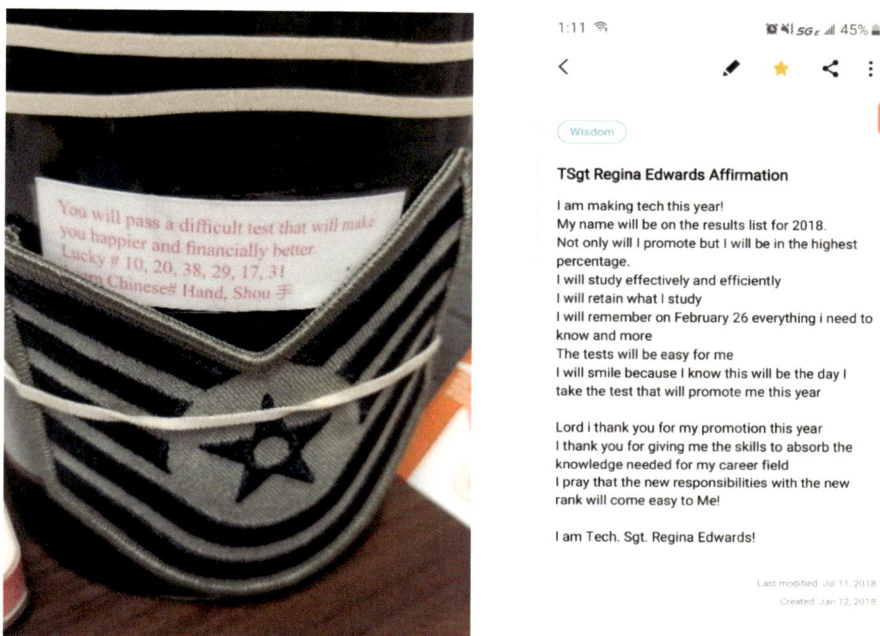

1:11

Wisdom

TSgt Regina Edwards Affirmation

I am making tech this year!
My name will be on the results list for 2018.
Not only will I promote but I will be in the highest percentage.
I will study effectively and efficiently
I will retain what I study
I will remember on February 26 everything i need to know and more
The tests will be easy for me
I will smile because I know this will be the day I take the test that will promote me this year

Lord i thank you for my promotion this year
I thank you for giving me the skills to absorb the knowledge needed for my career field
I pray that the new responsibilities with the new rank will come easy to Me!

I am Tech. Sgt. Regina Edwards!

Last modified Jul 11, 2018
Created Jan 12, 2018

(I took the test on February 26, 2018.)

Prayer/Vision Board

There was once a woman in my chain of leadership who was the human form of positive energy. First Lieutenant Kealy came to work with the most awkward stories, mom jokes that made only her laugh, and an inner electric nerve that wouldn't allow her to remain still for a significant amount of time. With all those traits, she made the office a better place to work.

Maybe her take on office energy came from a book she encouraged her subordinates to read, titled *The Energy Bus: 10 Rules to Fuel Your Life, Work, and Team with Positive Energy*, by Jon Gordon. I highly recommend this book for all aspects of your life. It changed my mindset.

During one of her training days with us, she asked about our goals, both personally and professionally. She told us to think about what we wanted and where we saw ourselves going, because knowing that affects the present and every part of your life that follows. She then gave us an assignment: Make a vision board.

I'd seen examples on social media, but I'd never done one of my own. She showed us her example, and of course, it didn't disappoint. It was filled with horrible drawings and art, but as she explained it, she mentioned there were items on her board that she already could mark off because they had come to pass.

"You may never start if you don't write it down and visualize it," she said. That made perfect sense to me.

> "And the Lord answered me, and said, Write the vision, and make it plain upon table, that he may run that readeth it." -Habakkuk 2:2

But why weren't more things happening for me? I wrote all the time. I wrote everything inside me… except my vision, except solutions. I wrote about my fears, my sadness, other people's opinions of me, and their effects, but not how I could overcome them. With this new insight from Lt. Kealy, I was excited about writing everything I believed my life would become in the future.

I created my first vision board sometime in July 2018. Some of the personal and professional aspirations were to: move from Arkansas (I was there for seven years, and left August 2018), get promoted (I found out I was selected for promotion July 2018 and the official promotion date was April 2019), learn how to swim (I started lessons August 2019 and was able to swim by October). These are just a few examples of what came to pass.

The lesson here is not in the board; it's in the courage to challenge yourself by writing out the thoughts for your life, and then daring yourself to realistically make steps to make it happen. We think about what we want all the time and how we want our life to bloom, but sometimes those dreams and goals stay buried underneath the soil of our hearts and eventually die because we didn't plant them properly, water or feed them. It's time to grab the pen, and then grab the shovel.

So many things grew in my life because I changed my perspective. My daughter witnessed the effects of my change, and she created a vision board for herself at the age of six. Several of her goals have come to pass as well. Jazzmyn has a YouTube channel called "Get, Get, Get It", where she inspires children to be themselves; she wrote that on her vision board. She has vitiligo and she wrote that she wanted her pigmentation to come back; it's coming back. She also wanted to do better at listening in school, and she has been a Pershing Hill General of the Quarter ever since.

With the success of our vision boards, my daughter and I decided to take it a little further. I created a prayer board in my room. When there is an issue, decision or situation, even if it's a request for prayers by others, we write the prayer on a sticky note, say a prayer out loud and place it on the board. Once the issue has been resolved, the answer for the decision has arrived, or a friend calls with good news, we move the sticky note over to the board beside that one(the answered prayers wall). We have seen cancer healed, behaviors changed, jobs offered, and not-so-good people's intentions revealed.

My daughter, who is now nine, loves these boards. She has become more confident in herself, and has increased her faith in God. She now knows that her words have power.

When we do her homework together, if she stumbles on a math problem, she stops and repeats this phrase three times: "I believe in myself, I believe in myself, I BELIEVE IN MYSELF" (the third time she yells it) and then she tackles the problem again.

At the age of eight, I knew nothing about confessing and affirming. I didn't know how to change the narrative. I'm so blessed that my daughter is equipped so early with tools I didn't know existed.

She is ahead of the game, and that's all I can ask for. I enVISION her growing up with confidence and self-esteem, no matter what obstacles come her way. She will be able to go through the trials of life, and when the boat is rocked and the mountains form, she'll pick up a pen, write out her affirmations and prayers, believe them, and then get to work.

And so will I.

After hearing how I learned to believe in what I felt to be true for my life, what do you believe you need work on affirming in yours? How can you take steps to manifesting some changes in your life?

What will you believe?

_____

_____

_____

_____

_____

_____

_____

_____

_____

_____

_____

_____

_____

_____

_____

_____

_____

_____

_____

_____

_____

_____

_____

_____

_____

_____

_____

_____

_____

_____

Chapter Four: Share your words

Iron sharpens Iron

I honestly never thought I'd reach a point in my life where I would be bold enough to bare all my truths publicly or feel worthy enough to actually believe that what I had to say was worth sharing. We all have a story to tell. We have all gone through something that can help another person along their journey. Many of us silently hurt alone because we think no one can relate to our pain.

I remember being in class, confused about what the teacher was saying. I wanted to raise my hand to get clarity, but fear and shame stopped me. Then all of a sudden, a classmate raised their hand and asked the very same question I was afraid to ask. Guess what happened next? No one laughed. The teacher didn't get frustrated for having to re-explain. That student wasn't less of person for not knowing. Along with that, every other student benefited from that student's boldness because we also got the answer to that question. I'm thankful for those people who were bold enough to raise their hands. They didn't do it for me, but their desire for self-improvement directly impacted me. I was a recipient of the knowledge their boldness generated.

This book is my hand raised for you. You may not be ready to share your story. You may still be searching for your own answers. That's absolutely fine. It took me thirty-two years to raise my hand and find my voice. I'll take this step so you can hear the answer too.

We are all at different stages in life. Each stage prepares you for the next.

The journey to believing in myself only came a couple of years ago. After my divorce and dating a psycho who took me to hell and back, I was at an all-time low. Moving to a new location was not the answer, but it helped me rebuild without any familiarities that could distract me or cause me to revert to old habits.

Listening to affirmations was my introduction into believing my words and realizing that I needed to learn another language. Negativity, guilt and shame used to be my native language, and whether you're a religious person or not, life and death are in the power of the tongue. You *will* become what you speak and what you constantly dwell on. When my language changed, my life changed.

When I was a young girl growing up in the country, unsure of myself due to being teased, all I had was my love for writing and using words to express my thoughts. No one ever saw them. I never read them to anyone. It was just me and my words. They were my therapy. They were my friend.

Becoming a teenager and, later, a young woman, I grew tired of crying in the bathroom or the back of the school bus. I was tired of smiling at friends who I knew had just talked behind my back. It was time to stand up for myself. The fear and shyness were still there, but every once in a while, when I had more than I could take, I would speak my mind and it felt good!

People were shocked at these few moments of outbursts throughout the years and almost offended that I had the nerve to speak up, but I *did* have the nerve. I was slowly—very slowly—gaining confidence in myself. It was a different feeling, but it felt like home. It felt like that young girl was back. The girl who didn't think she was ugly. The girl who thought her full lips and high cheekbones were special and unique. I was becoming a woman evolved, and it was reviving.

Write your words. Even if you never tell that family member they hurt you, if you never reveal your secret crush, placing your thoughts on paper can help you release emotions and help you organize your thoughts.

Speak your words. Not only the negative or the confrontational. Tell yourself you're beautiful. You're worthy. You're enough. Tell yourself you got this! And mean it!

Believe in yourself. It starts with you. Let's stop extending grace and love to everyone around us, but holding ourselves to completely unrealistic expectations. Repeat after me:

"I believe in myself! I believe in myself! I BELIEVE IN MYSELF!!" (Thanks, Jazzmyn!)

And now we're here: the biggest challenge for me by far. My life finally feels balanced. I'm in a healthy relationship with myself first (which is most important), my finances are in order, my family dynamic is great, and my small circle of friends is beyond a blessing to me.

I'm writing, speaking and believing. I wanted to pat myself on the back and move on, but God said no. I didn't go through all of that to keep it closed in a diary. These lessons weren't just for me. I had to share them.

This piece of my heart would not have been available to you if it weren't for divine intervention. God spoke to me in so many ways and through so many people that there was no doubt I had to complete this vision.

One person in particular is definitely owed honor for his obedience to do what he was called to do. He is not my pastor, and we have never met, but he is a gift from God.

On January 8, 2019, during my nine-hour drive home to South Carolina, I decided to go to YouTube and listen to Pastor Mike Todd of Transformation Church in Tulsa, Oklahoma. I had begun following him during his "Relationship Goals" series, and have watched just about everything his ministry has done since. During that drive, I listened to "2019 Vision//Release," which had been published the day before, as well as "Bring me Another Vessel," which was published in 2018.

In those sermons, I heard the commands, "release" and "write the vision." I had been going to church my whole life. "Write the vision; make it plain" is a verse in the Bible (Habakkuk 2:2) spoken quite often, but it never sat in my spirit like this before. The whole drive, God whispered thoughts to me.

"You're going to write a book. Tell your story."

I couldn't wait to stop the car and write all these ideas in my notebook. I felt like God was over my shoulder, whispering in my ear, telling me exactly what the book would be about, what it would look like, and whom it would reach. I never in my life wanted to write a book, but in that moment, I knew I could do it, I would do it, and I was meant to do it.

Pastor Todd said "2019 is the year of release, and on the other side of release is freedom." He explained I would have to disconnect from habits, people and mindsets in order to reach my next level of purpose. Not only would I have to be released *from* things, but I also had to accept that it was time to be released *into* a new chapter.

As I was driving and receiving this new revelation, Pastor Todd literally said in his sermon, "If God is telling you to release the book, why wouldn't you do it?"

He continued to say that releasing also means to make something public. You make it known so you can help someone else along the way. My mind was blown. I got chills, and that was the confirmation I needed.

In another sermon, Pastor Todd said, "We sometimes discount what we have and call it insignificant, but what we're counting *out* is what God is counting *on*! God says all you have is all I need. Go back to sharpening your gifts and skills, and stop burying them."

I've been writing my whole life. In school when we had to write stories and poems, people would always say they always enjoyed my writing, but I still kept it to myself as much as possible. Writing had been my personal and private gift, and I wasn't ready to unlock my pages completely.

When I joined the military, the first thing I did was become a sexual assault victim's advocate. For nine years now, I've been providing support to people affected by all forms of sexual trauma. As introverted as I am, people (even strangers) have always stated they feel safe enough to talk to me about their problems.

It seemed as if God had been grooming me my whole life for this moment. I had to go through struggles. I had to overcome challenges, heal inner hurts, and defeat demonic giants in order to have experiences and wisdoms to share because "all things work together for the good of those who are called and love God." (Romans 8:28)

Since I've started writing this book, I've joined forces with a military peer and together, we've created a "Let's Talk" forum where other like-minded people come together and share experiences on life, love, race, culture, purpose, trauma, healing and so much more. Every time we get together, I feel like I'm sharpened even more. I've become wiser, more compassionate, more open minded, more unbiased but most of all more free—free to tell my truth, free to see a goal that may be unattainable to some but believe I can do it, and free to love and be loved.

When you hear the call to share your words, step out on faith and share them. You'll never know the thousands and tens of thousands of people waiting for your story to set them free. I am so grateful for the people who were obedient at the appointed time so a sad, insecure young woman could hear God speak through them.

Their iron sharpened my iron, allowing me to use my **W.O.R.D.S.** not only as **W**eapons **O**ver **R**eal-life **D**ecisions and **S**ituations, but also **W**eapons **O**ver **R**egret, **D**epression and **S**hame!

This may be the end of one chapter in my life, and definitely the end of this book, but it is only the beginning for this journey. If me going through what I experienced has helped you in any way, then we are forever connected. Your path may not take you to these realizations in the same order as my path did for me, and that's perfectly fine. You may pick up this book in several different stages throughout your life. However, I pray that it will bring you clarity and wisdom as you need it.

Life gets hard. We lose hope at times. We fail. We forget who we are. We love and don't receive it back. We begin to believe the lies at times. Those are all true.

But what is also true is, we are extraordinary beings. We are loved. What we possess is enough. Trouble is temporary. We are not defined by our failures and mistakes. Life is beautiful, and we only get one.

What will you do with yours? Who will you impact? What legacy will you leave? What do you have to say to the world?

What will you share?

Think about those things. Meditate on them. And when you're on your journey of discovering the answers, remember to write it, speak it, believe it and share it.

Love you all.
God bless,
Regina Farai' Edwards